Sunlight Growing

We all need more sun

Dale Allman

- We as humans are conditioned to need the outdoors. Our bodies, minds and spirits benefit when we stay connected.

- Many of the exact same benefits from being outdoors do occur from simply looking at nature. A dedicated time – even a few minutes – when we focus on pictures, photos or videos of natural scenery reaps many benefits.

- All photos used are licensed for commercial use, under Creative Commons license.

- Sources of the latest research include:

  - Comments and health-related perspectives taken from Business Insider, April 2018, Kevin Loria, "Benefits of being outside…"

    - 12 reasons why it's good to be outdoors

  - "Among office workers, even a view of nature out a window is associated with lower stress and higher job satisfaction.

  - "Vitalizing effects of being outdoors", Journal of Environmental Psychology, June 2010, Richard Ryan (first author)…

  - "Looking at photos of nature (just 20 minutes a day) can chill you out"…

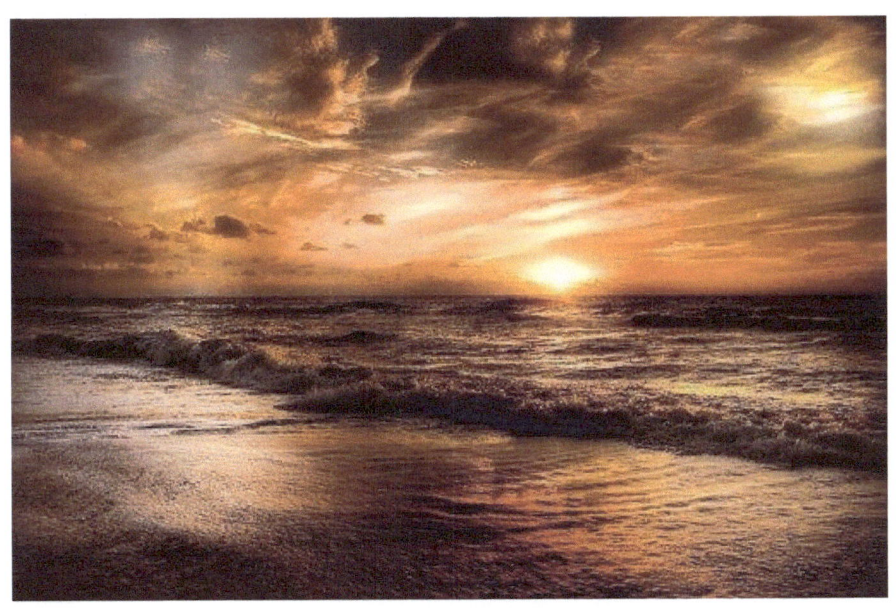

Sun light growing when new days begin.

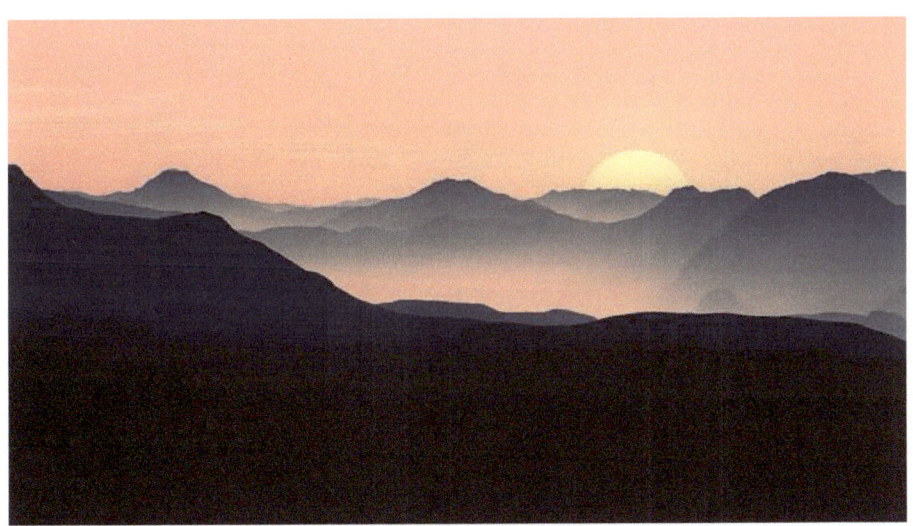

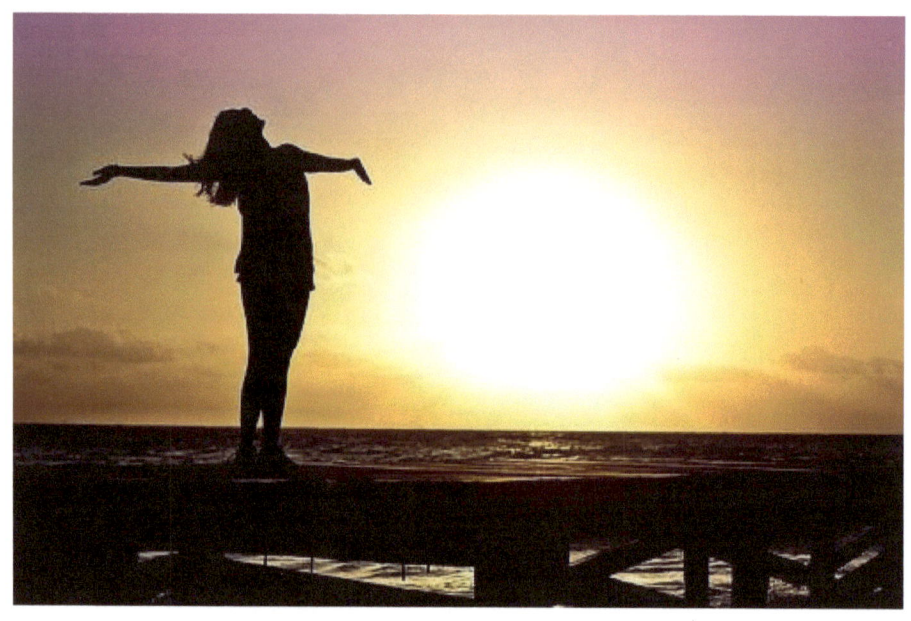

Greet the new day you and your city

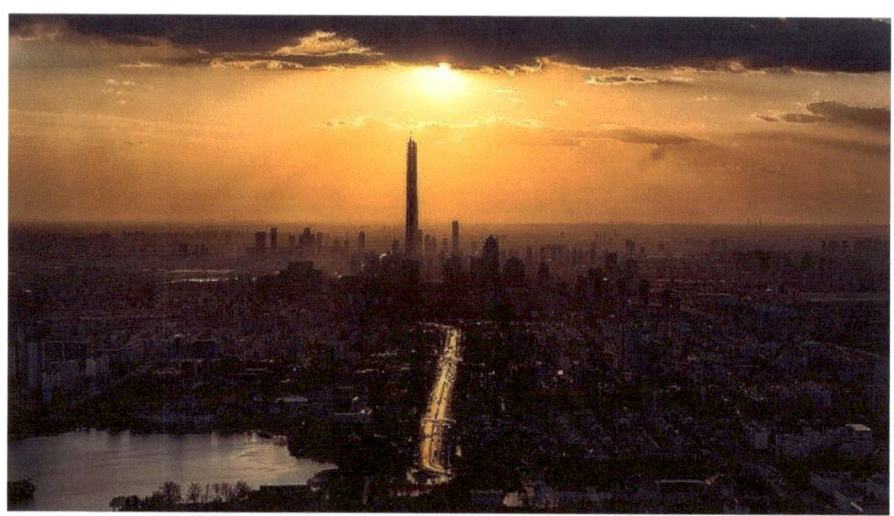

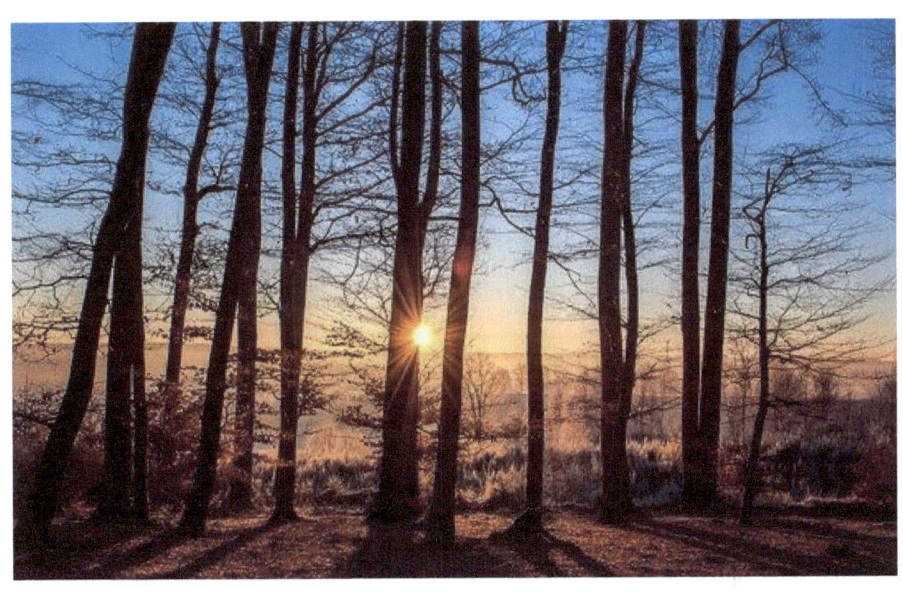

Explore the wonders around you

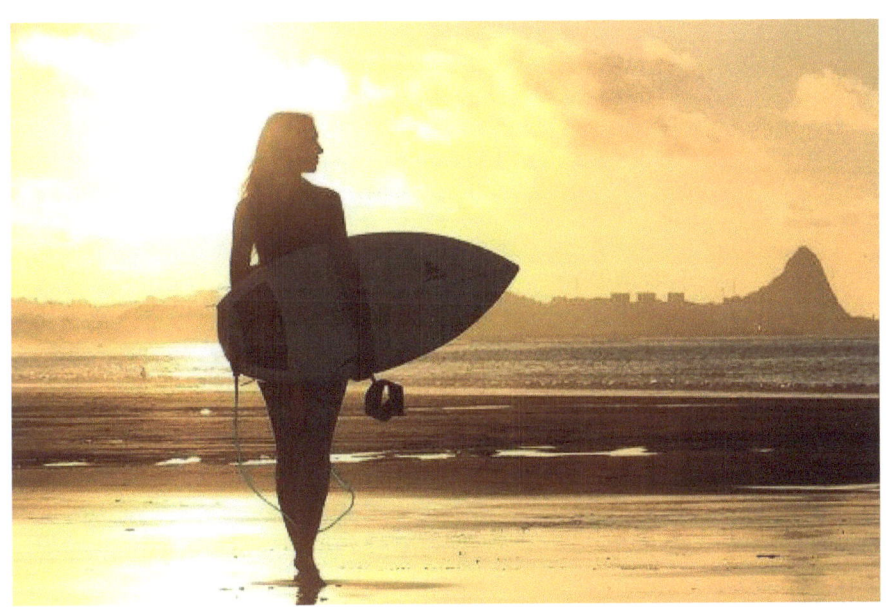

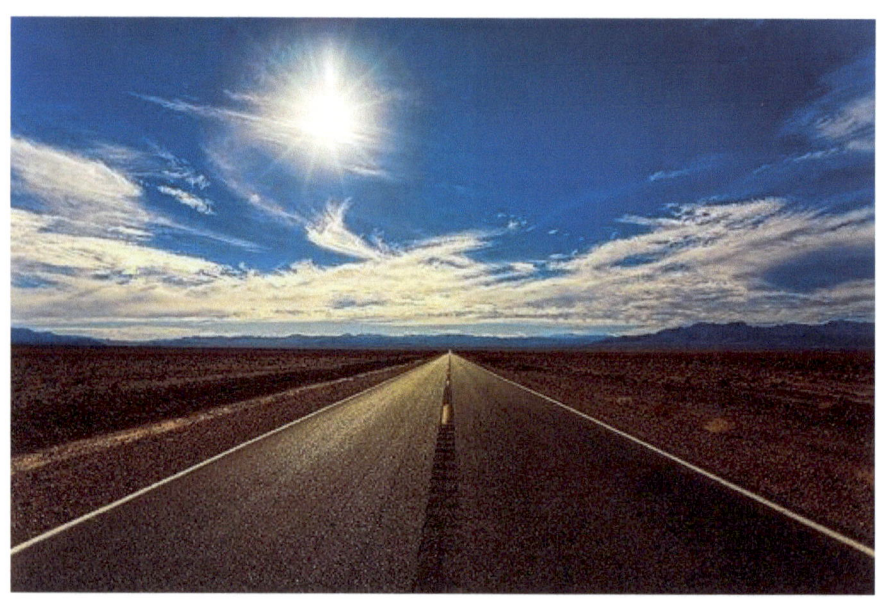

Get there however you can

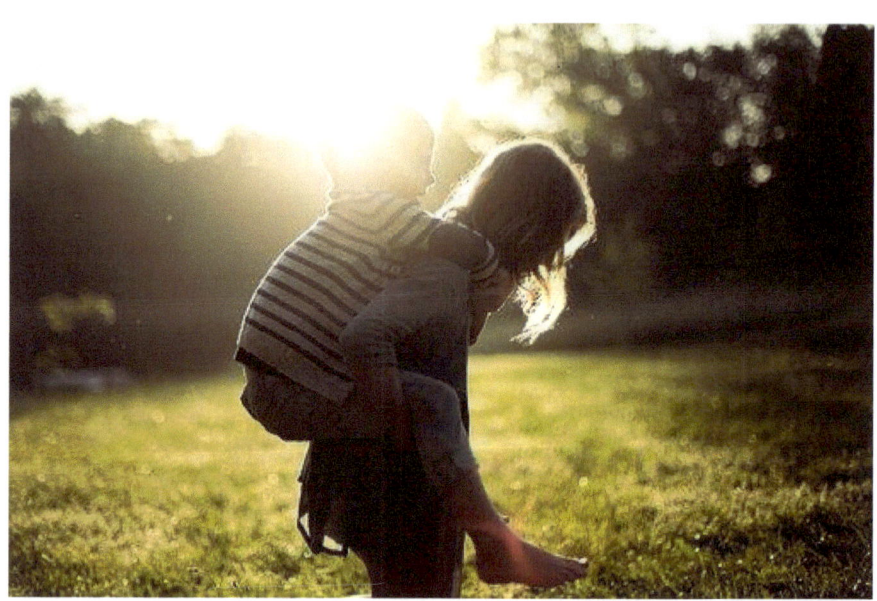

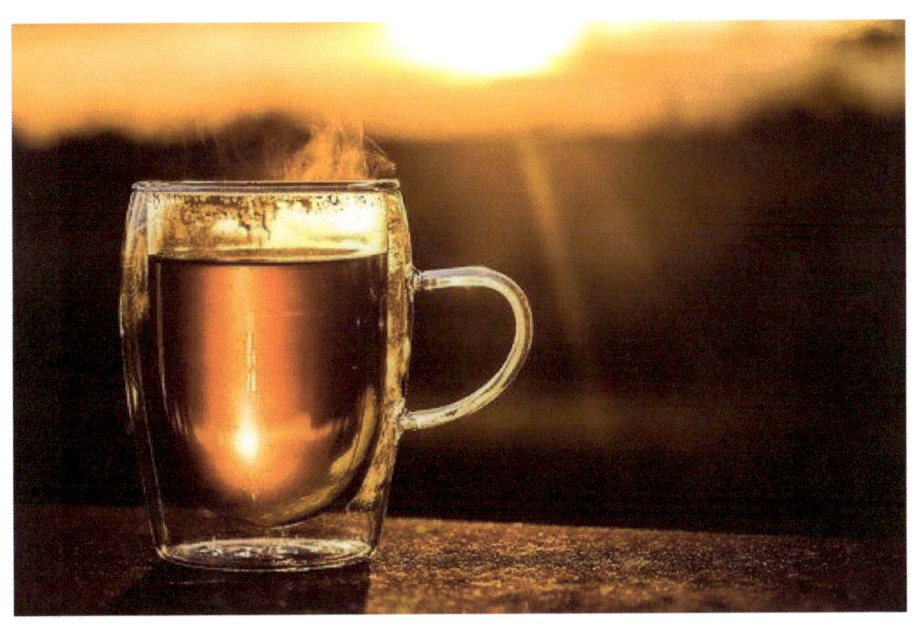

But stay close to the light

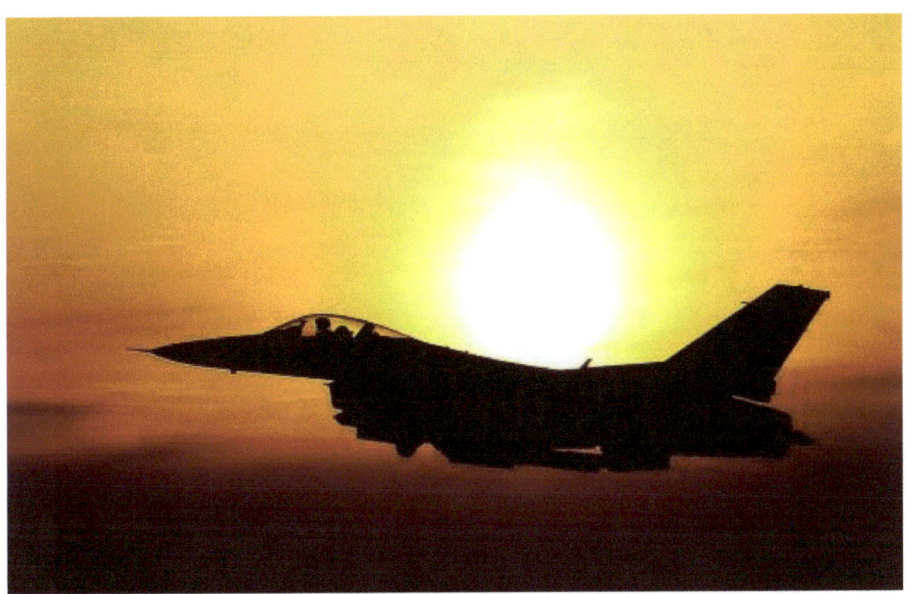

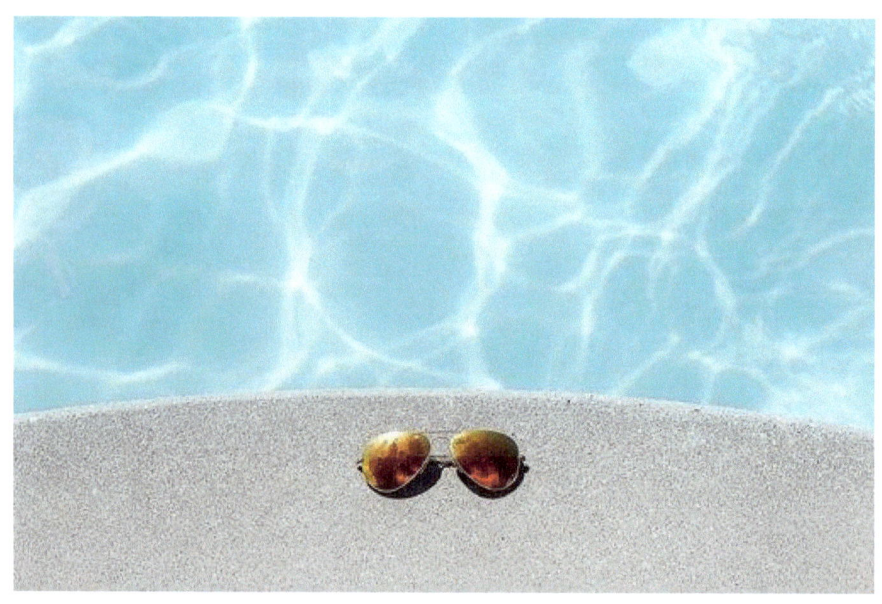

Even if you have to leave

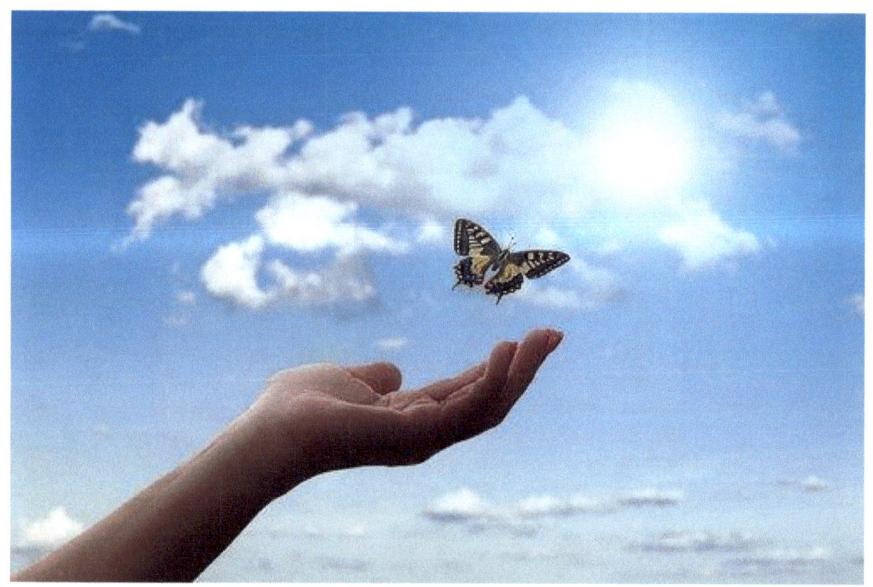

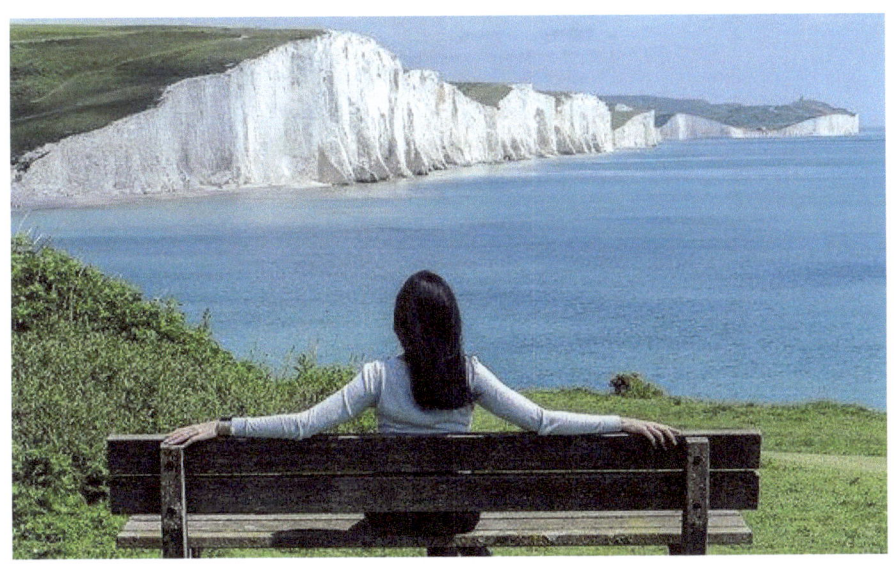

Always come back

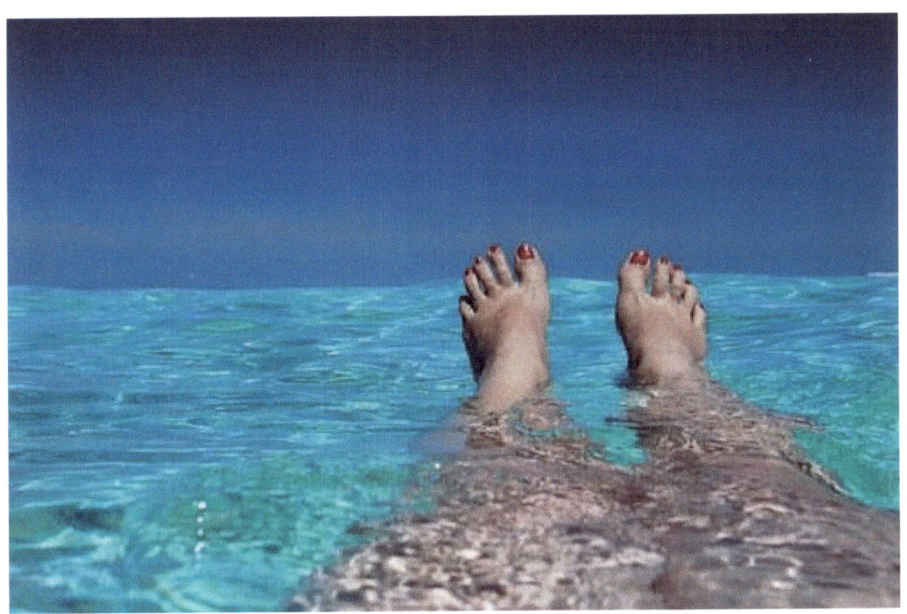

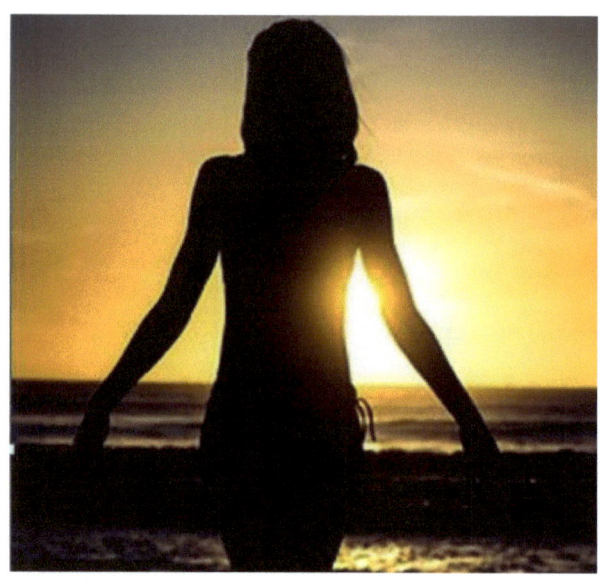

Release yourself to the light

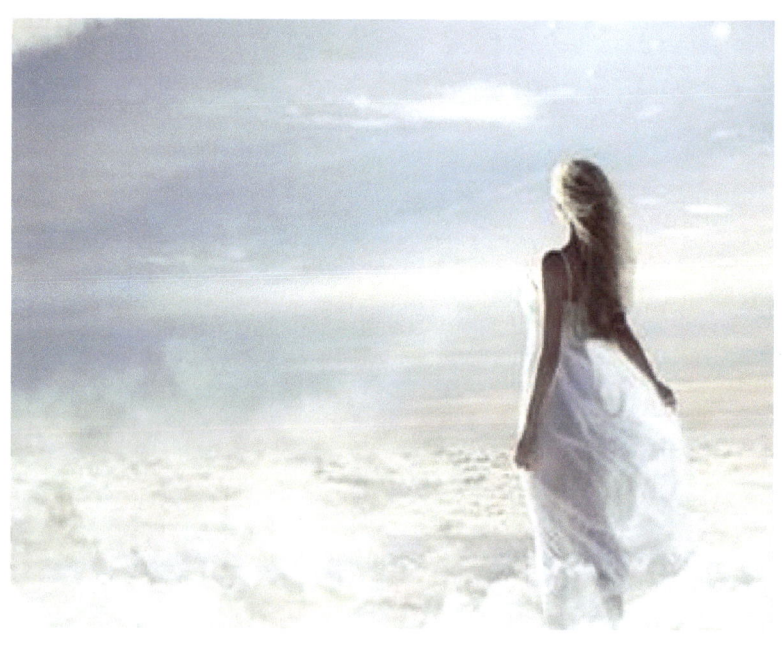

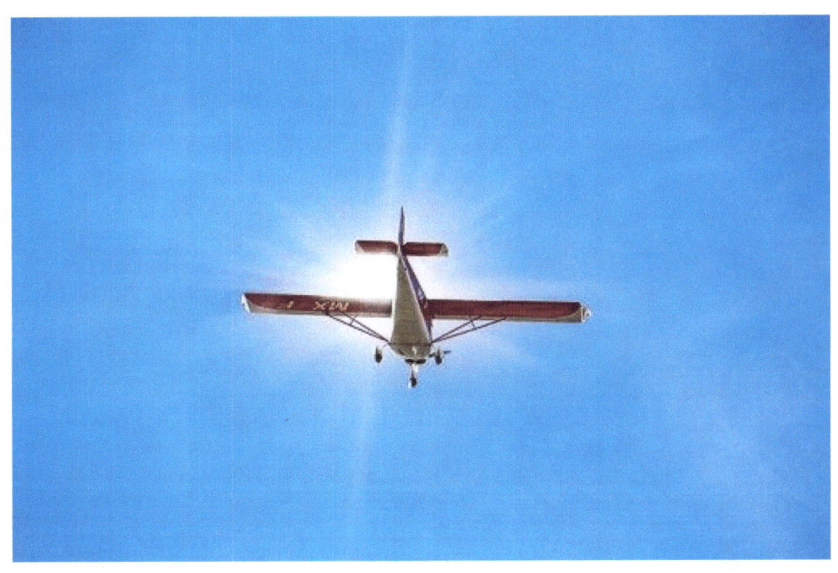

Work in the sun

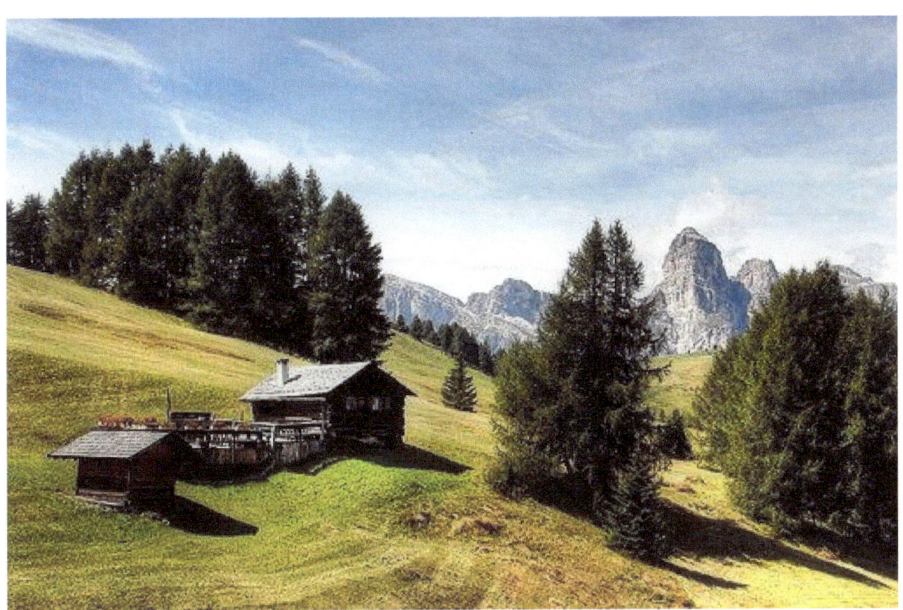

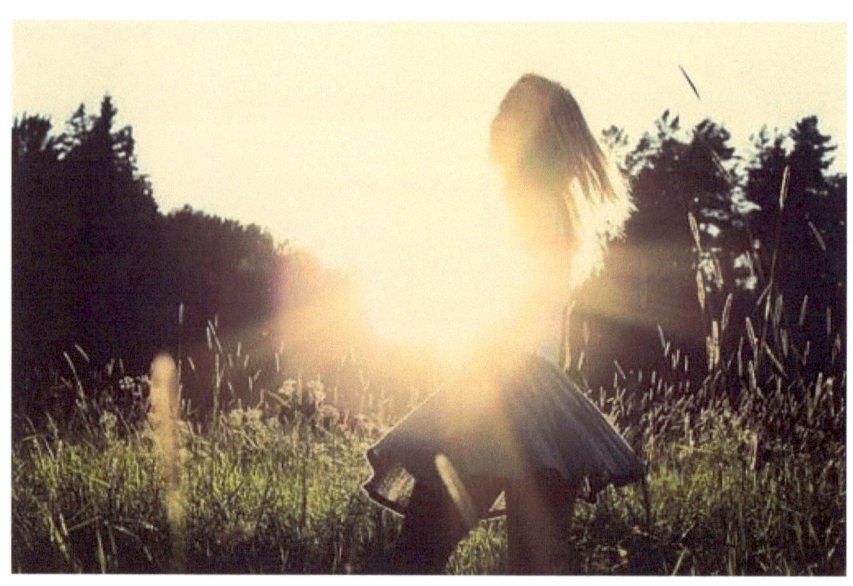

Dance in the light

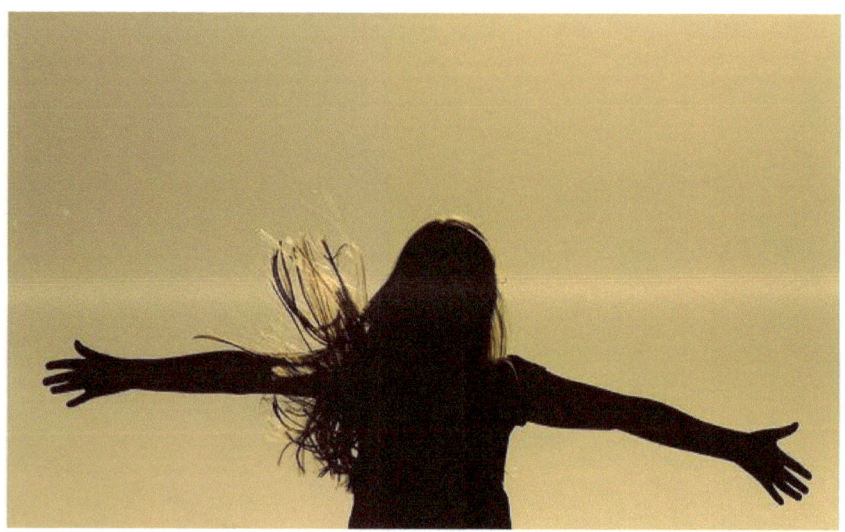

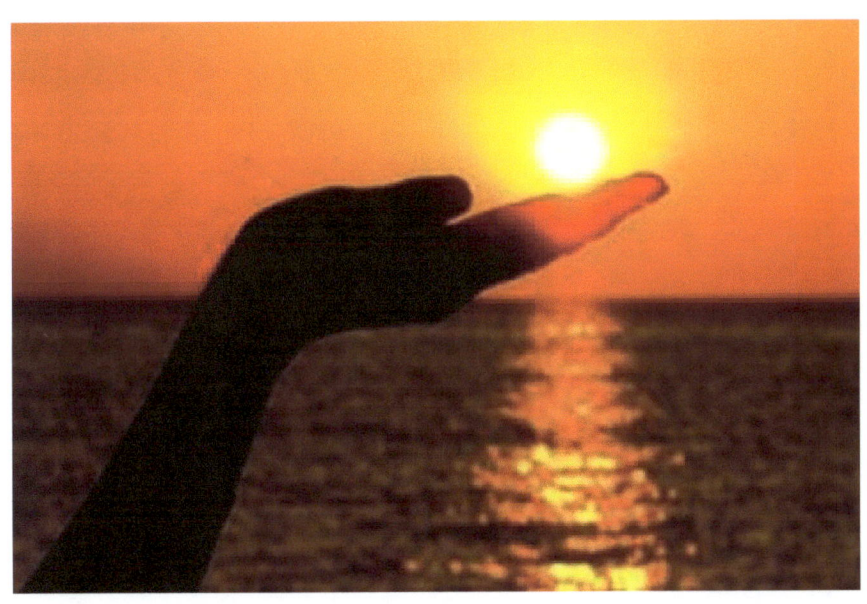

Play with the light

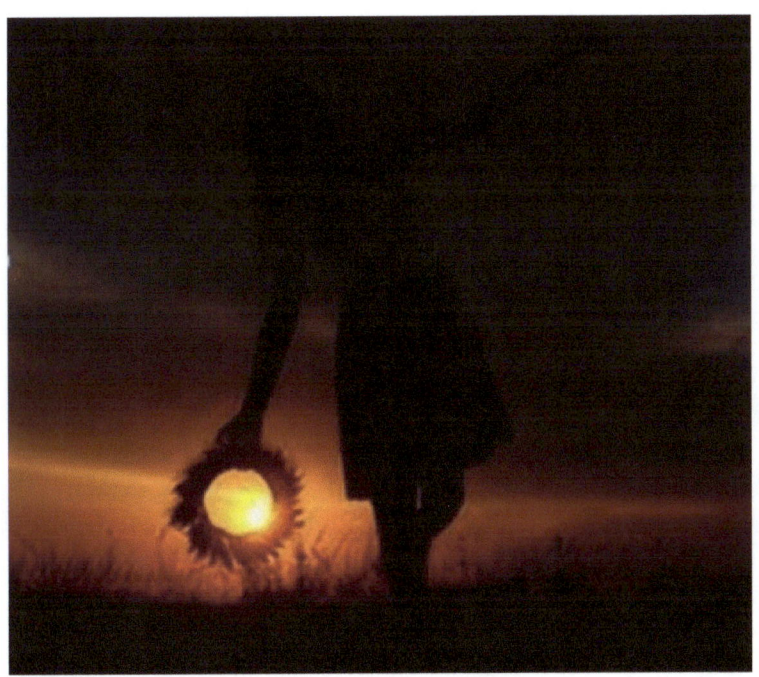

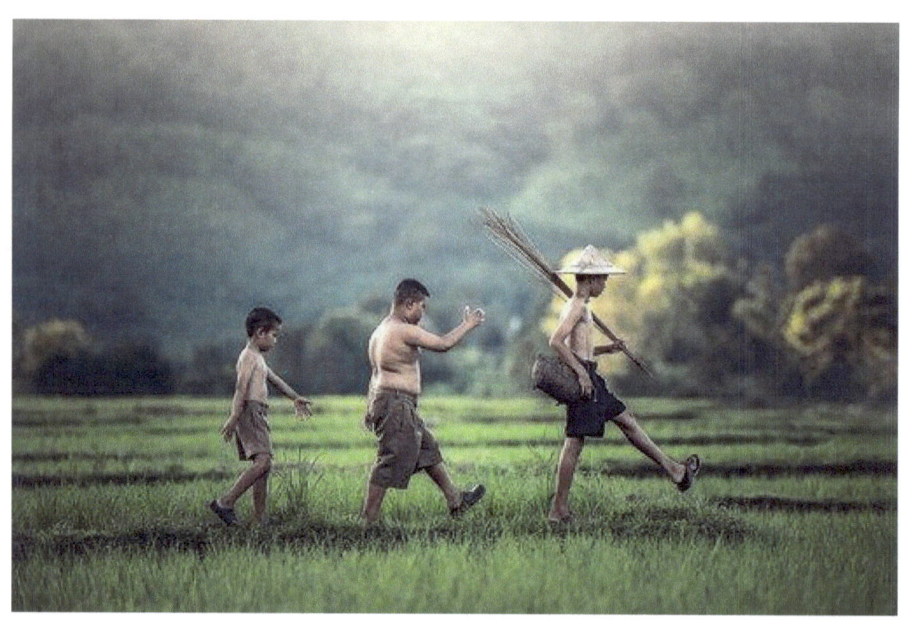

Work and play in the light

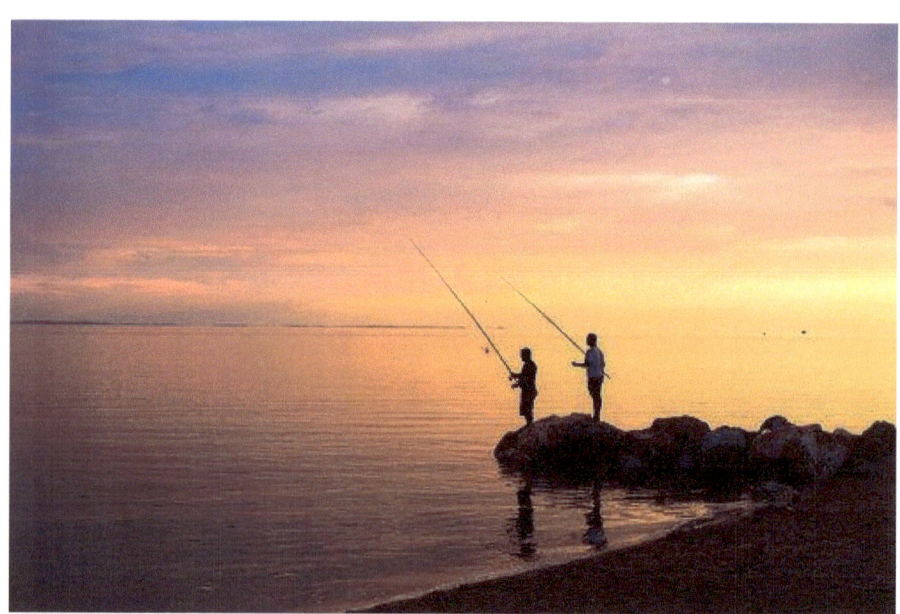

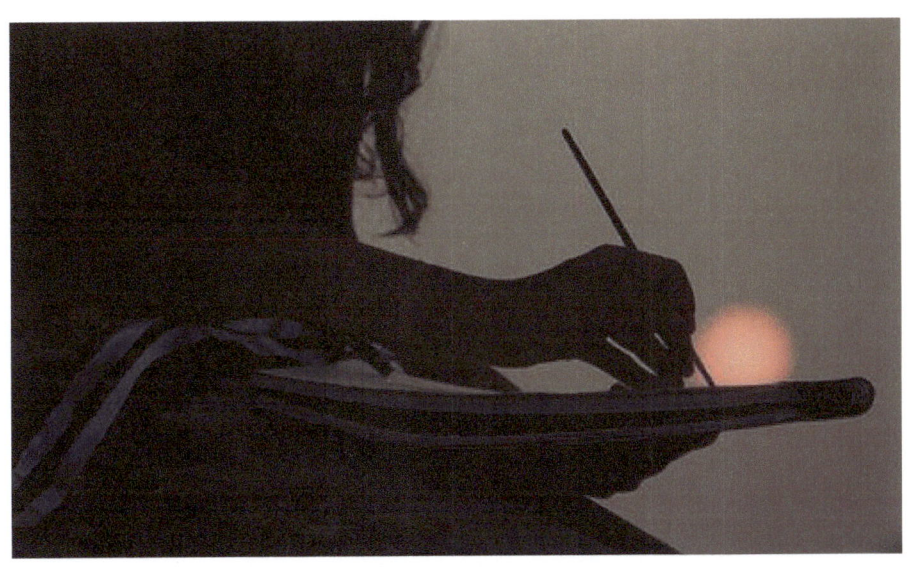

Use the last of the light

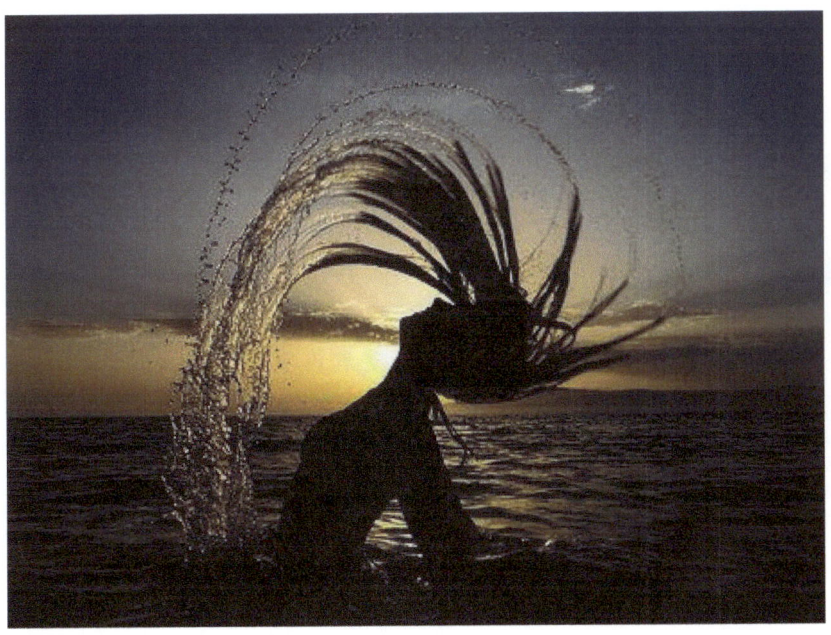

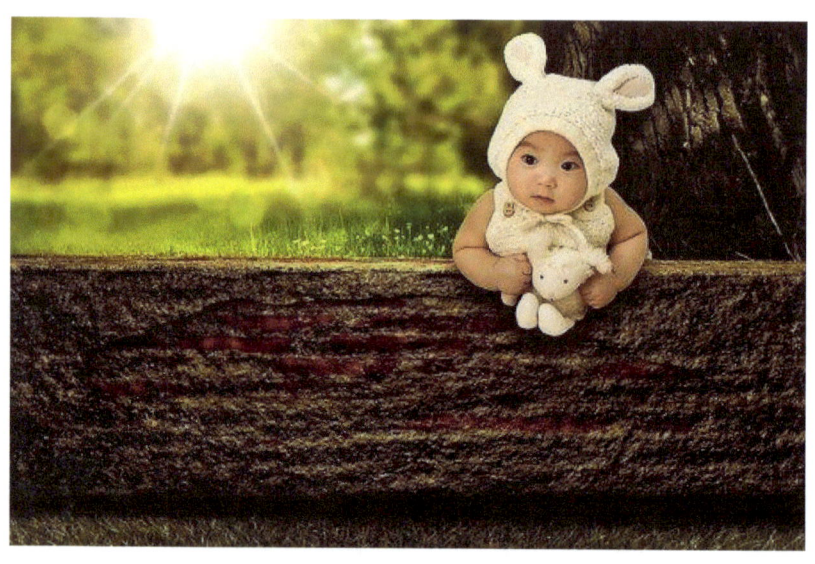

Add beauty to the light

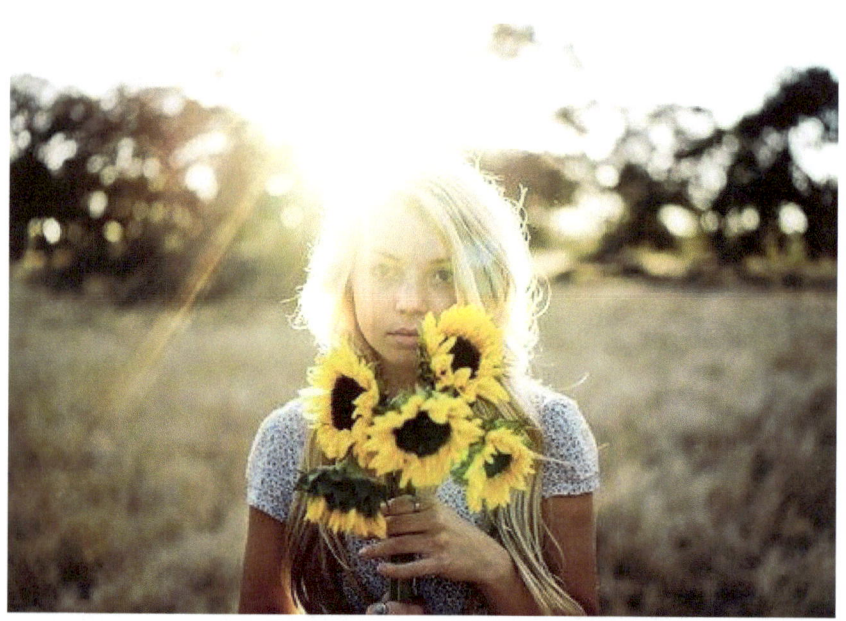

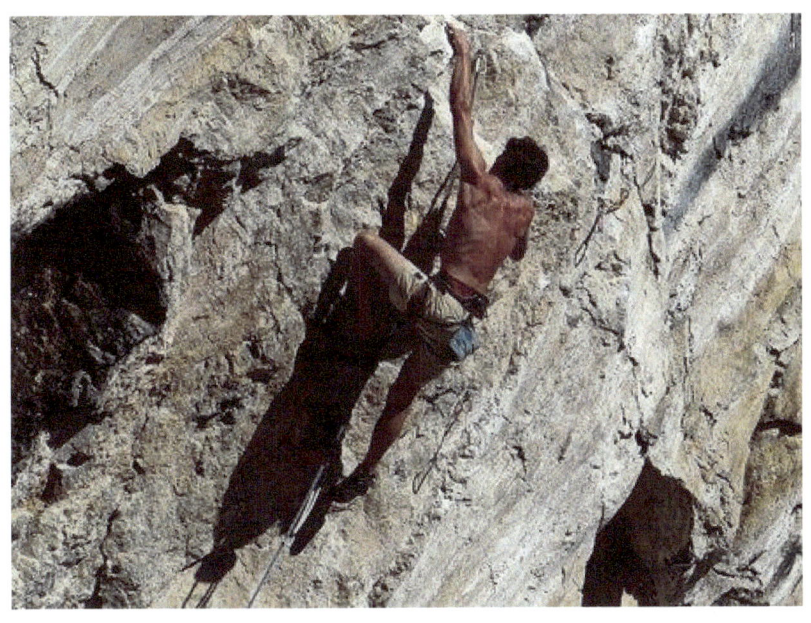

Climb toward the light

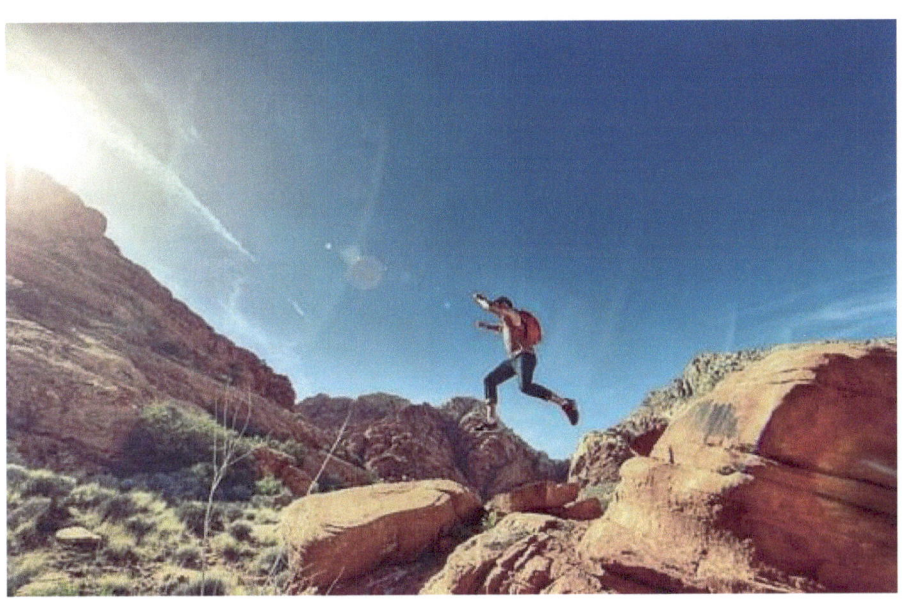

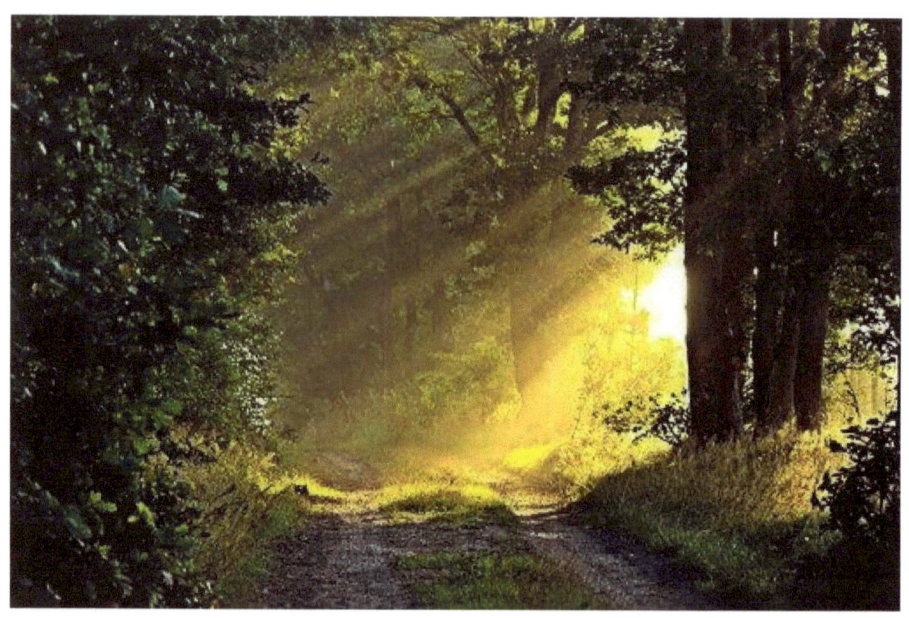

Explore new places with the light

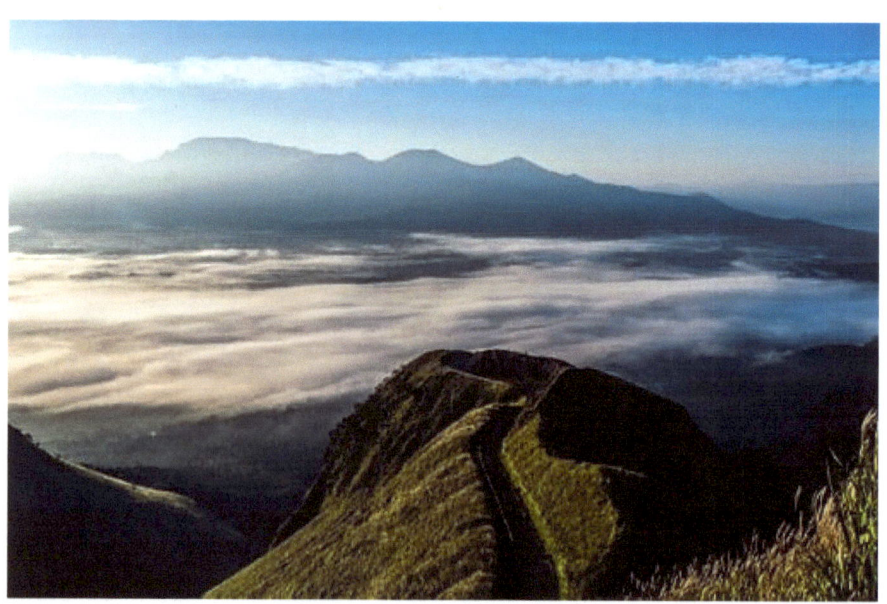

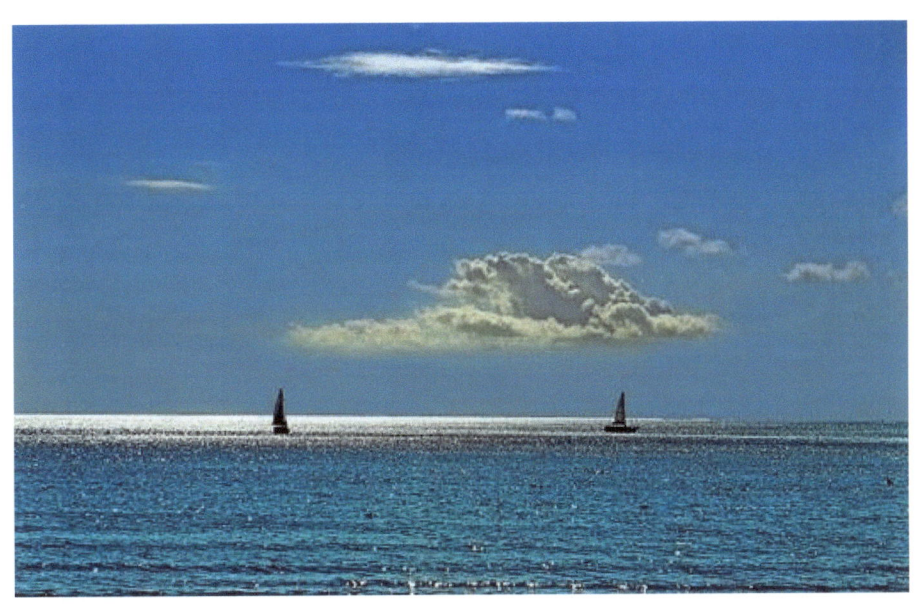

Get farther from the shore

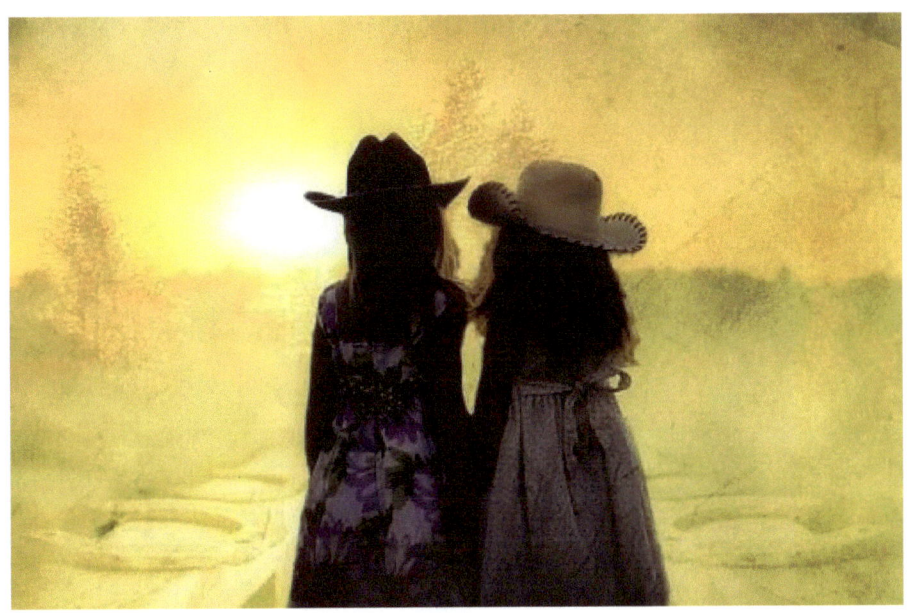

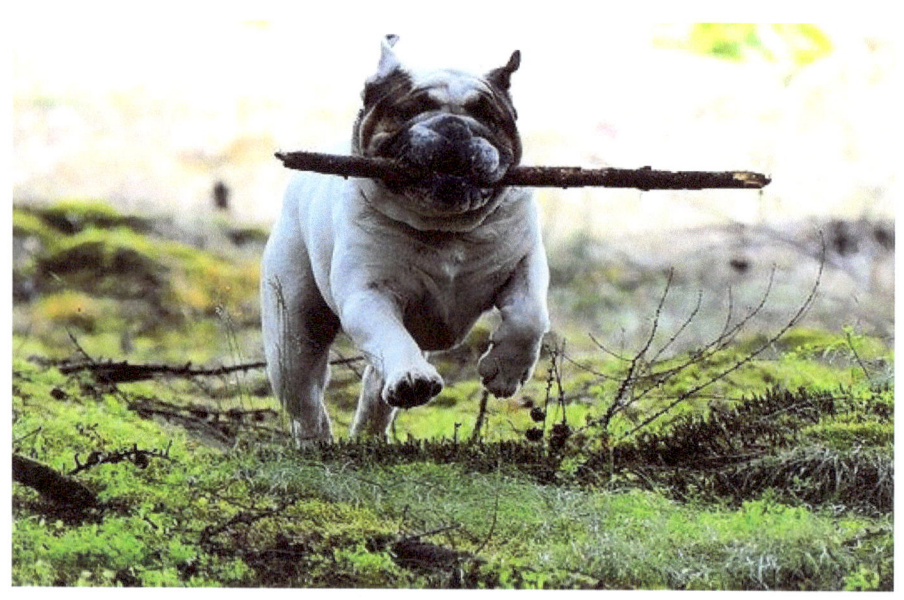

Play with friends in the light

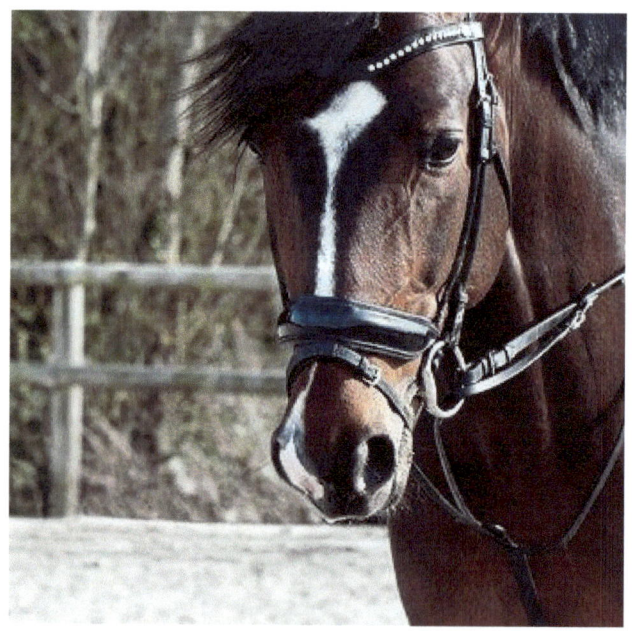

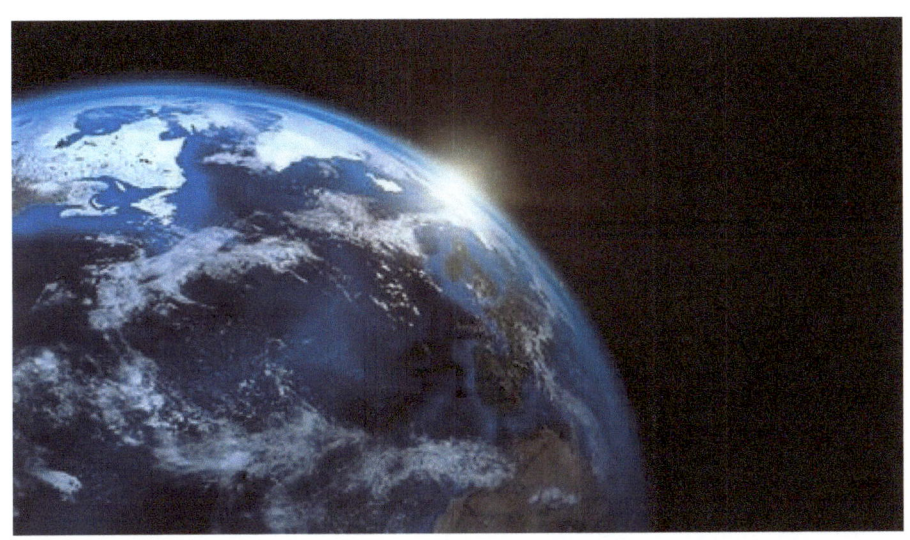

Think big in the light

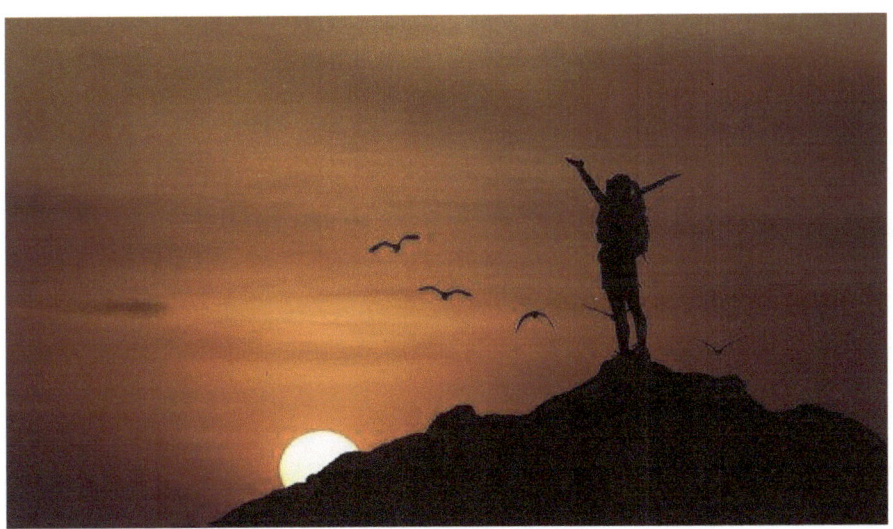

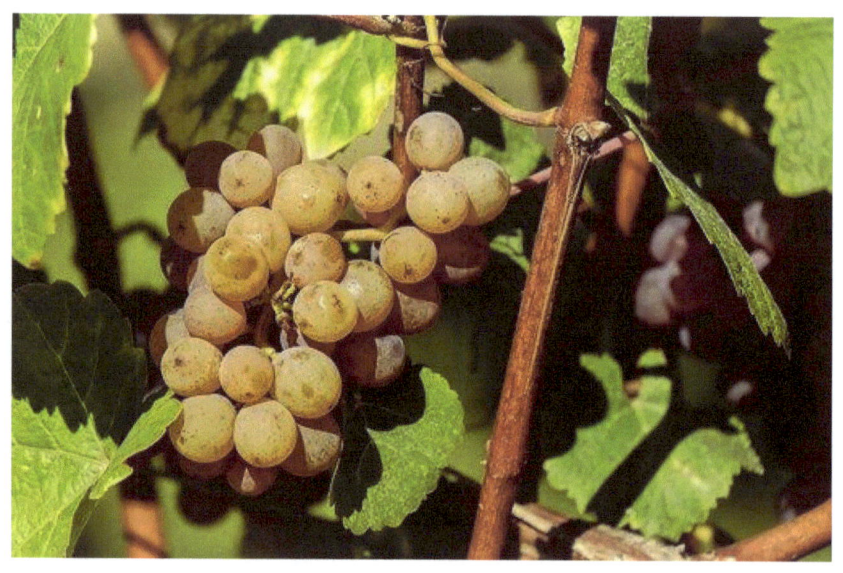

The light nourishes us all in many ways

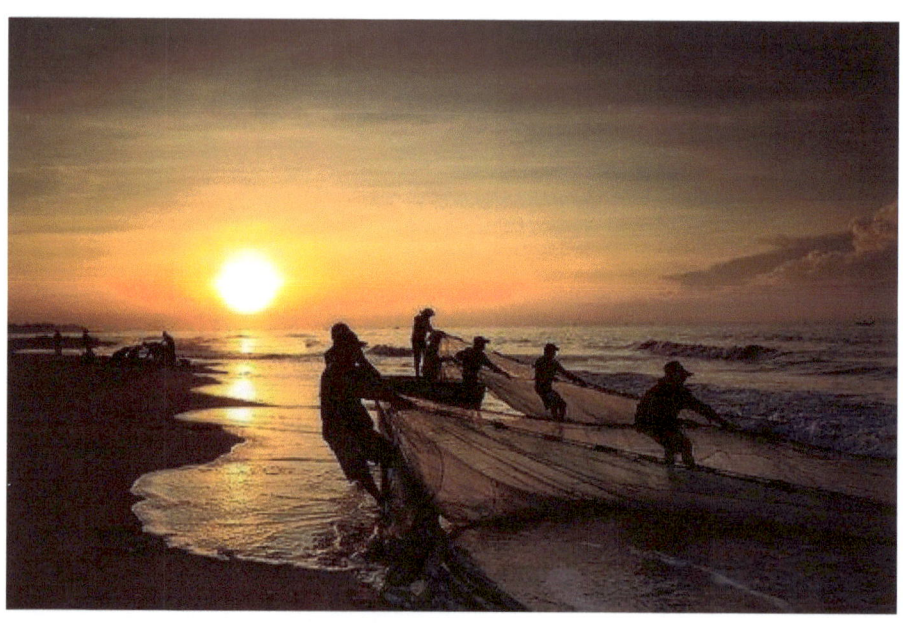

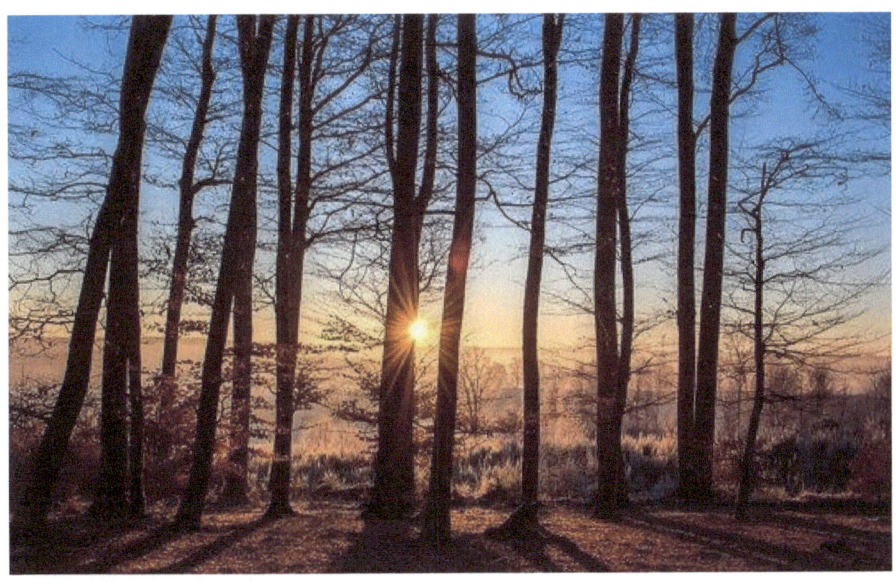

Look beyond the light

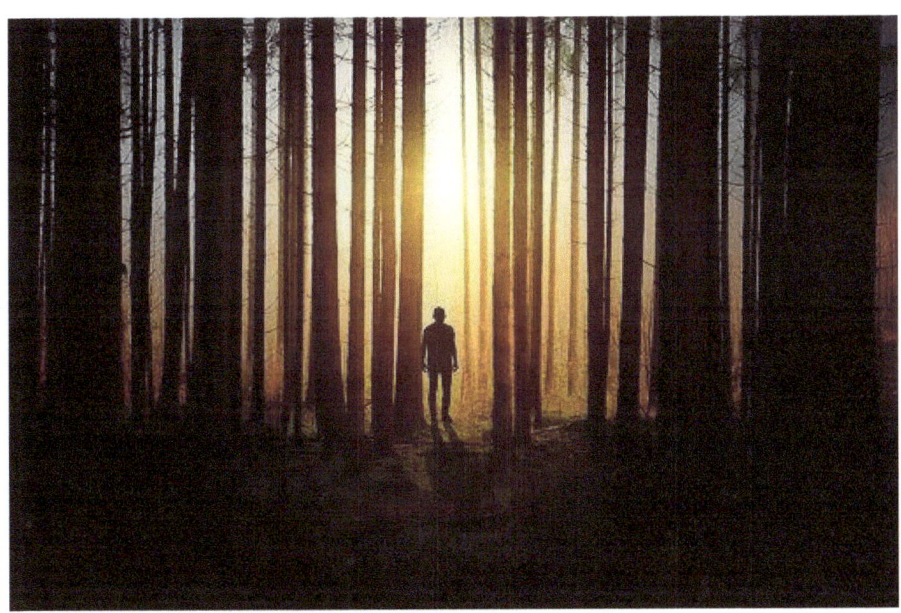

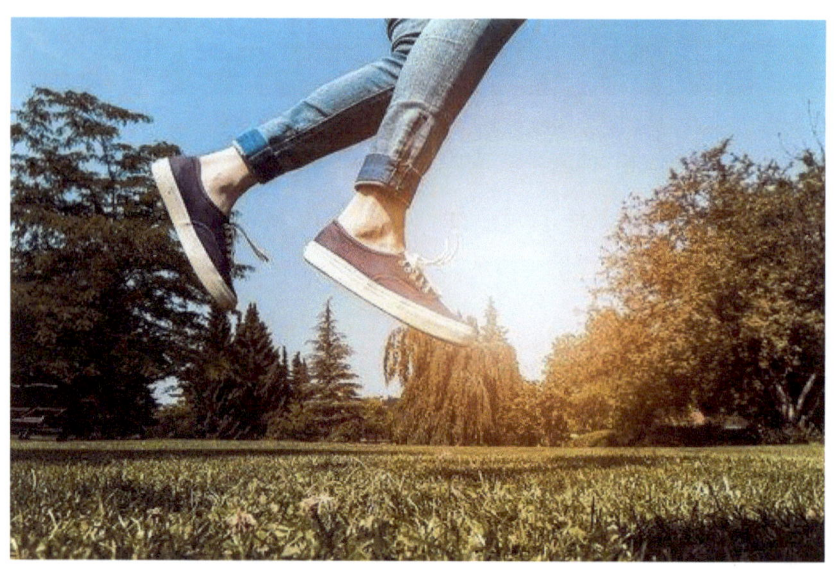

The air and the light are your friends

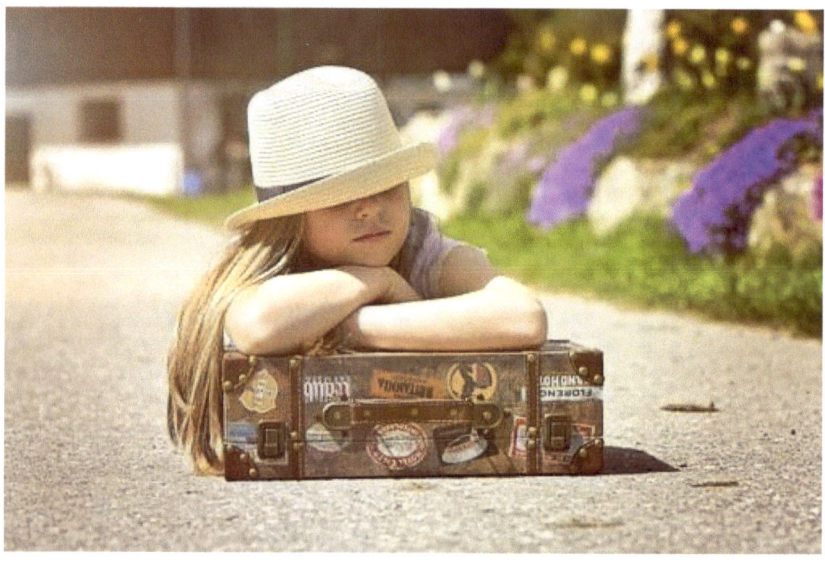

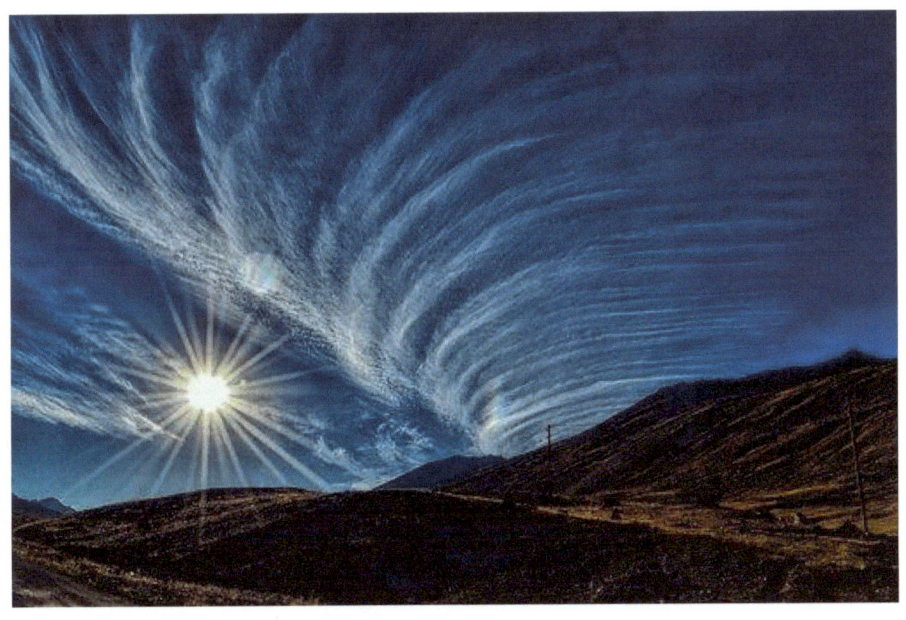

Paint the world with your light

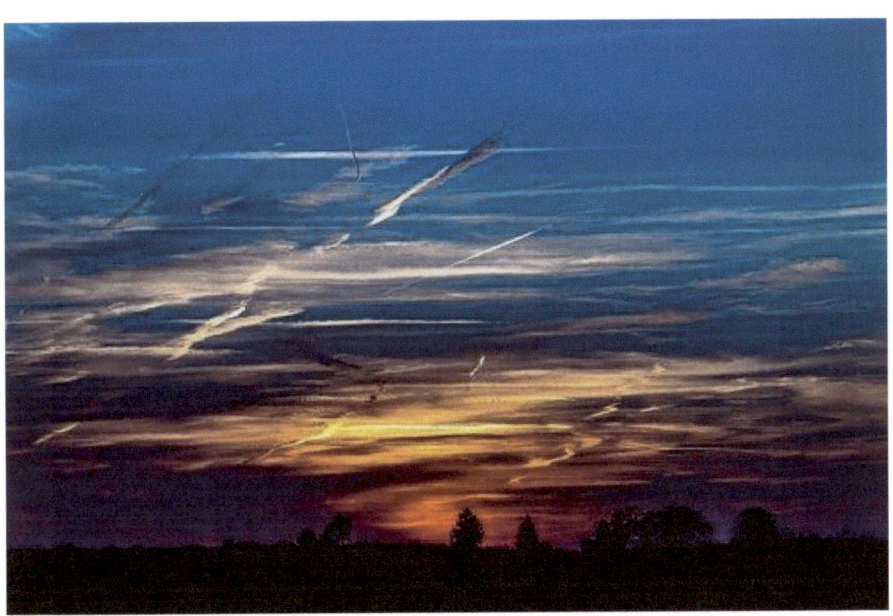

Sunlight Growing

Copyright 2018. All rights reserved.

Now available on Amazon.com for high-quality (HQ) printing.

www.ingramcontent.com/pod-product-compliance
Lightning Source LLC
Chambersburg PA
CBHW040306220526
45473CB00002B/596